Defend Your Life III

ALSO BY SUSAN REX RYAN

The Eyes Have It

Defend Your Life II

Silent Inheritance

Defend Your Life

Defend Your Life III

Vitamin D and Immunity

Susan Rex Ryan

DISCLAIMER

The purchaser or reader of this book hereby acknowledges receiving notice of this DISCLAIMER. The author and SMILIN SUE PUBLISHING, LLC, publisher of this book, are not engaged in providing medical care or services, and the information presented in this book is in no way intended as medical advice or as a substitute for medical counseling. The information in this book is not intended to diagnose or treat any medical or physical condition or problem. If medical, professional, or other expert assistance is needed or required by the reader of this book, please seek the services of a competent expert. This book is based upon information taken from sources believed to be reliable. Although reasonable caution has been taken in compiling the information contained herein, this book may not contain the best or latest information and, in fact, may contain mistakes. The reader should use this book only as a general guide. The opinions expressed in this book are not to be relied upon as statements of fact. Anyone who reads or purchases this book, or any vitamin, mineral, or supplement mentioned in this book, acknowledge that they are relying upon their own investigation and not on any statements or opinions expressed herein, and are making their own independent decisions after discussions with their doctor or other medical professional. This book is sold without representation or warranty of any kind, express or implied, and the author and SMILIN SUE PUBLISHING, LLC are not liable or responsible to any person or entity for direct or indirect loss, damage, or injury caused or allegedly caused by information contained in this book.

Published in March 2022 by Smilin Sue Publishing, LLC.

smilinsuepubs.com

ISBN Print: 978-0-9845720-9-0
ISBN eBook: 978-0-9845720-4-5

Book design by BookWise Design.
Cover image by wildpixel.

Dedication

To those who endeavor to improve
their health—easily, safely, and effectively.

CONTENTS

INTRODUCTION

"Why another vitamin D book?" you may ask. I felt obliged to inform my readers about recent information on the effectiveness of vitamin D's synergistic relationship with immunity. Specifically, I have read enough scientific literature on human studies about vitamin D's role involving COVID-19 to compel me to share the medical world's findings with you.

Let me make clear: supplementing with vitamin D is not the panacea for preventing and treating COVID-19. And I know there are varying approaches to protecting against, and combating, this highly contagious virus and its variants. Nonetheless, the medical literature suggests that vitamin D may play a role in immunity for catching and treating contagious pathogens such as coronaviruses.

Defend Your Life III serves several purposes for you, the reader.

The initial part of this book offers a review of the basics of vitamin D. Part I addresses the fundamentals of this helpful vitamin including its various sources as well as biochemical partners. Furthermore, the comprehensive testing chapter provides information including laboratory reference ranges of partners and substances associated with vitamin D.

Part II is the heart of this book. First, I address immunity, a complex subject, in easy-to-understand language. Second, the next chapter focuses on the vitamin's role in immunity. Third, there are chapters about vitamin D's role with immunity-related respiratory viruses such as COVID-19, influenza, RSV, and the common cold.

The third part of *Defend Your Life III* addresses vitamin D's function in prevention and treatment. This part offers a selection of how vitamin D mechanisms of action may affect aging, cancer, diabetes, and oral health.

Of course, the popular Vitamin D Wellness Protocol is included in *Defend Your Life III.* This document describes how, by supplementing daily with vitamin D and two other partners, you may increase your vitamin D levels. Tens of thousands of individuals have used the Protocol, many of whom report a healthier way of life.

I sincerely hope you find *Defend Your Life III* informative and useful. For our new readers, welcome to the amazing world of vitamin D!

~Susan Rex Ryan

PART I

Vitamin D 101

1

VITAMIN D REVIEW

Less than fifteen years ago, the words "vitamin D" were rarely uttered by members of the general population. Today "vitamin D" is almost a household word.

Despite its relative popularity now, the concept of vitamin D has been around since ancient times. For example, Hippocrates, the father of modern medicine, used sunlight exposure to treat a type of tuberculosis.

More than a thousand years later, rickets, a disease characterized by soft and disfigured bones, emerged in Europe. Caused by vitamin D deficiency, this malady was initially documented in England in 1650. During the nineteenth century scientists began understanding the positive effect of ultraviolet B (UVB) sunlight on treating rickets. By the early twentieth century solariums were popular across the globe to treat diseases including rickets, tuberculosis, and rheumatism.

We discuss vitamin D and its significant connection to sunlight in the next chapter.

Now let's look at vitamin D basics. We know that vitamin D is technically a steroid hormone, produced by our bodies when we: expose our skin to UVB light; consume large quantities of fatty fish or vitamin D-fortified foods; or take a vitamin D3 supplement.

Unless you bask daily in UVB rays under the optimal conditions stated in Chapter 2, consume immense amounts of wild-caught fatty fish, or follow the daily Vitamin D Wellness Protocol stated later in this book, you might have inadequate levels of vitamin D that may increase your risk of developing an array of medical conditions.

Many people—across generations and geographic locations—suffer from deficient vitamin D levels because their lifestyles do not usually include vitamin-D-rich foods, unprotected sunbathing, or taking the proper supplements.

- A study published in *The Journal of the American Osteopathic Association* found high vitamin D deficiency prevalence worldwide. Two osteopathic doctors conducted a comprehensive review of vitamin D including its physiology, deficiency risk factors, diagnosis, and treatment. They found that about one billion persons globally, or nearly fifteen percent of the world's population, have a vitamin D level of less than 30 ng/mL, well below the optimal level of 100 ng/mL.

Symptoms of low vitamin D include a host of common complaints such as muscle weakness, fatigue, bone pain, and chronic back pain, as well as susceptibility to contagious illnesses such as COVID-19. Vitamin D deficiency is easy to diagnose by a simple blood test (please see Chapter 4) and treat by taking three over-the-counter supplements daily.

Let's understand the basic process of vitamin D in the body. Our health is controlled and maintained by trillions of cells, the smallest units in the human body. The body's organs comprise millions of cells. Cells contain components called receptors that control what vitamins, minerals, hormones, and other substances (medications, free radicals, etc.) can enter or depart a cell.

Vitamin D receptors (VDR) receive and, in some cases, produce activated vitamin D. VDR are present from head to toe: in our brains, hair follicles, eyes, and skin as well as in, *inter alia*, our cardiovascular, endocrine, gastrointestinal, immune, musculoskeletal, nephrological, neurological, reproductive, and respiratory systems.

The most natural way to obtain vitamin D is from moderate exposure to UVB rays from the sun. When your skin absorbs UVB rays, your body interfaces with a chemical called 7-dehydrocholesterol and produces **initial** vitamin D (cholecalciferol). Alternative sources for vitamin D are cholecalciferol from over-the-counter supplements and limited foods.

It is interesting to note that cholecalciferol is included as an "essential medicine" in the World Health Organization's (WHO) Essential Medicines List (EML). The EML "contains the medications considered to be the most effective and safe to meet the most important needs in a health system."

Once cholecalciferol is produced in the skin cells, it enters the blood stream and travels to the liver. The liver processes—by hydroxylation—vitamin D into **circulating** vitamin D (calcidiol or 25-hydroxyvitamin D).

Circulating vitamin D travels along two distinct paths. First, the kidneys convert calcidiol into activated vitamin (calcitriol or 1,25-dihydroxyvitamin D). This activated vitamin D interacts with the parathyroid glands to maintain calcium blood levels.

Second, if circulating vitamin D remains in your bloodstream after calcium levels are maintained, the liver converts the leftover circulating vitamin D into activated vitamin D. The "excess" activated vitamin D travels in the blood to your tissues and cells and attaches to VDRs to perform functions essential to improved health:

- Fight viral and bacterial infections.
- Regulate gene expression.
- Reduce inflammation.
- Regulate cell differentiation, proliferation, and natural death (apoptosis).

These mechanisms of action are vital to protecting you from developing a wide array of medical conditions including autoimmune disorders, cancer, and osteoporosis.

How Safe is Vitamin D Supplementation?

Vitamin D toxicity is rare. As you have learned, vitamin D supplementation mimics the production of cholecalciferol in your body when UVB rays strike your skin. Scientific studies indicate that our bodies can naturally absorb about 20,000 IU (international units) from daily exposure to UVB rays to make enough vitamin D to protect us from most illnesses. I take 20,000 IU daily to thwart contagious illness and maintain my overall health. Chapter 6 elaborates on how effective adequate vitamin D is to bolster the immune system.

Furthermore, a 2019 study in Ohio reported that, after seven years of over 4,700 psychiatric patients supplementing with vitamin D3 (either 5,000 or 10,000 IU a day), there were no issues with calcium and parathyroid levels. "Due to disease concerns, a few patients agreed" to supplement with 20,000 to 50,000 IU daily! The researchers concluded in the *Journal of Steroid Biochemistry and Molecular Biology* that "long-term supplementation with vitamin D3 in doses ranging from 5,000 to 50,000 IU a day appears to be safe." Therefore, a daily vitamin D supplementation of about 10,000 IU, specified in the Vitamin D Wellness Protocol, is safe for most people.

Please note that persons who suffer from kidney and/or liver disease, or hyperparathyroidism, should consult a medical practitioner before taking vitamin D supplements. In addition, folks who are using cardiac glycosides or thiazide diuretics should check with their health care provider prior to using supplemental vitamin D.

Concluding Thoughts

Vitamin D is a steroid that is produced when cholecalciferol is in the body. Sources of cholecalciferol are UVB light, a limited number of foods, and over-the-counter supplements. Cholecalciferol is recognized by the WHO as an essential medicine under "Vitamins and Minerals."

Too much vitamin D in the body is rare. Nonetheless, the safest method of controlling your vitamin D supplementation is to monitor through blood testing your circulating vitamin D and calcium levels at least every six months until you have achieved a vitamin D status that you wish to maintain.

In the next chapter we address the primary sources of vitamin D.

2

SOURCES OF VITAMIN D

The most natural source of vitamin D is exposure from the sun's UVB rays. The sun has provided its light including UVB rays as long as we have inhabited the earth. People originally lived and worked outdoors. They wore little, if any, clothing. And they lived near the equator, the closest distance to the sun.

Fast forward to the Industrial Revolution in the nineteenth century, two twentieth-century world wars, vast technological advances, and global economic markets. Today people live and work indoors. They commute and travel by enclosed conveyances. Air conditioning has become widely used at workplaces and in homes. These lifestyles have contributed to vitamin D deficiency.

Let's briefly review a decades-old campaign launched by the cosmetic industry. Seeking additional revenue, the cosmetic industry endeavored to market its products as not only beauty but "health" aids. In the 1970s, the cosmetic business reportedly began funding medical schools' dermatology departments with the intent to influence the American Medical Association (AMA) to educate the public about the dangers of sunlight. In 1989, the AMA issued the warning that caused millions to purchase and apply sunscreen and sunblock products. Well, you know the rest. The sunscreen business totals in the billions of U.S. dollars, and the sun scare continues today as does the prevalence of vitamin D deficiency.

Outdoor UVB Light

We do not need to hide our skin from the sun. The body possesses an inherent mechanism to produce vitamin D from the sun. The skin can produce about 20,000 IU of "intake" vitamin D a day depending upon several situational factors.

After the body acquires enough D (usually about 20 minutes of ideal UVB exposure), the skin's safety mechanism turns off the initial production of vitamin D. Moderate exposure to the sun is healthy.

A number of factors affect the degree of UVB sun rays absorbed by our bodies to produce vitamin D including:

- *Geographic location.* Location is paramount to making vitamin D in your skin. The closer to the equator (lower latitudes), the higher the altitude, the better opportunity to acquire vitamin D-rich sunlight.

- *Time of day.* The higher the sun is in the sky, the better to obtain vitamin D from the sun. The hours of 10:00 AM to 2:00 PM local time are the best times to get vitamin D from direct sunlight. If your shadow is shorter than your height, you are in a potential vitamin D-producing window.

- *Season.* Many medical studies have demonstrated seasonal effects on vitamin D levels. The sun shines the longest period during the summer and the shortest timeframe during the winter.

- *Cloud cover.* An azure sky is highly preferable to cloud cover. UVB light is decreased by about 50 percent when penetrating cloud cover.

- *Air quality.* An adverse product of industrial civilization is ozone pollution, which absorbs UVB sun rays before they can reach your skin.

- *Age.* The older one is, the more challenging it is to obtain and maintain adequate vitamin D levels from sunlight. As people age, the concentration of the vitamin D precursor (7-dehydrocholesterol) in the skin decreases.

- *Weight.* Overweight and obese people have difficulty producing adequate vitamin D. As vitamin D is fat-soluble, the body's fat cells absorb this essential nutrient, decreasing its availability to the organs, tissues, and cells.

- *Skin pigmentation.* Melanin, the pigment in your skin, absorbs UVB rays. The darker your skin color, the more difficult it is to make vitamin D in your skin. People with darker skin may require up to 10 times the sun exposure that light-skinned people need to produce vitamin D. African Americans have staggering rates of low vitamin D and accompanying incidences of medical conditions associated with vitamin D deficiency.

- *Glass windows.* Sunning by a glass window or door may feel soothing but it will not help you make vitamin D. Glass eliminates at least 95 per cent of UVB light.

- *Sunscreen and cosmetics.* The marriage of cosmetics and sun protection factors (SPF) will reduce the ability for skin to make vitamin D. The application of either product to your skin most likely will block UVB sunlight.

- *Clothing.* Not only are we encouraged to "cover up" in the sun but some clothing including swimwear contains SPF chemicals! The more clothing we wear in the sun, the less vitamin D is produced in our skin.

Indoor UVB Light

Optimal conditions for producing vitamin D from the sun are dependent on a few elements. Some factors we can control, and others we cannot. So, what about using indoor sources of UVB light to produce vitamin D in our skin? For almost a century, UVB lamps have been used to treat medical conditions.

Decades later, tanning beds became popular. People tend to frequent tanning facilities to look better, e.g., sport a tan during the winter. However, can the use of tanning beds increase vitamin D levels? The answer is “it depends.” Having toured tanning salons, I found that most beds do not use UVB light. (Ultraviolet A lights are the most common bulbs in tanning beds, but they do not stimulate vitamin D production.) If you are using a tanning facility, ask specifically for a bed that only provides UVB light.

Using indoor UVB light is an individual choice. Personally, I have not been inclined to utilize indoor tanning. I opt for limited, outdoor UVB exposure and oral vitamins D and K2 supplementation.

Food

Many Western diets are not rich in fatty fish caught in the wild. Foods that naturally contain vitamin D include salmon, mackerel, sardines, and cod liver oil. (However, cod liver oil contains a large amount of vitamin A, potentially disrupting vitamin D's processing. Please see Chapter 3.)

A number of foods are enriched with vitamin D, or cholecalciferol. Common vitamin D-fortified foods in the United States and the United Kingdom are milk, cereals, and fruit juices but they only contain small amounts of vitamin D. Enriched foods most likely will not effectively treat a vitamin D deficiency because large quantities of these foods would need to be consumed daily. For example, you would need to drink ten eight-ounce glasses of vitamin D-fortified milk daily to obtain merely 1,000 IU of vitamin D.

Vitamin D Supplementation

The most practical and effective treatment of vitamin D deficiency is to take a soft gel or liquid drop containing vitamin D3, in accordance with the Vitamin D Wellness Protocol addressed later in this book. Quality vitamin D supplements are readily available online or over-the-counter in retail stores.

The one truly effective vitamin D form is called vitamin D3 or cholecalciferol. Activated vitamin D3 is the bioidentical substance that our bodies recognize to perform essential health functions that include strengthening bones to decreasing the risk of developing cancer, autoimmune diseases, and other serious medical conditions.

For decades, a less effective form called vitamin D2, or ergocalciferol, has been used in supplements as well as food and beverage fortification. Vitamin D2 contains synthetic compounds that are chemically altered and not well recognized by the body. Despite these facts, vitamin D2 can still be found in enriched foods and beverages as well as multi-vitamins and other supplements.

When selecting a vitamin D3 supplement, please carefully read the ingredient labels on vitamin supplements and fortified food and beverages to ensure you are buying D3—the only "real" vitamin D!

Beware of Prescription Vitamin D

Misperceptions about treating vitamin D deficiency still abound among medical practitioners and their patients. When treating patients for almost any medical condition, many conventional medical professionals "automatically" write prescriptions—the perceived "holy grail" for effective treatment. In turn, patients usually salute smartly by taking the prescription. However, in the case of treating vitamin D deficiency, beware of prescriptions.

At least in the United States, vitamin D deficiency is often treated with a *prescription* for "vitamin D." Guess what? The prescribed vitamin D usually contains the less effective form of vitamin D2 (ergocalciferol) that I addressed above. Patients usually take one *prescribed* 50,000 IU capsule a week, for about eight to twelve weeks. Most patients however are completely unaware that prescribed vitamin D2 comprises synthetic compounds that are chemically altered and not well recognized by the body. In my opinion taking a vitamin D *prescription* is like trying to fit a square peg into a round hole; the square peg simply does not fit! Prescribed vitamin D2 most likely will not improve your levels. Therefore, your vitamin D deficiency will not be effectively treated. You most likely will not feel better and will be wasting your time and money.

Vitamin D3 Soft Gels and Liquids Are Better Absorbed

Vitamin D is dissolved in fat. Therefore, vitamin D3 supplements in soft gel or liquid form are absorbed better than chalky tablets or chewable, fructose-laden pills. The best time to take your vitamin D3 supplement is right after your breakfast. Healthy fats, including olive oil, egg yolks, and avocado, will facilitate the absorption of vitamin D3 in your body.

Concluding Thoughts

Vitamin D supplementation is easy, effective, and inexpensive. In the next chapter you will see other nutrients that work closely with vitamin D.

3

VITAMIN D'S PARTNERS

Vitamin D does not function alone in the body. Other vitamins and minerals interact as cofactors with activated vitamin D and perform the essential functions explained in Chapter 1. Fat-soluble vitamin K2 is dependent upon fat-soluble vitamins A and D's functions. The minerals calcium, magnesium, phosphorus, zinc, and boron also team with vitamin D.

Carefully read this chapter. The fact that specific vitamins and minerals function effectively with vitamin D does not mean that you should begin (or modify) taking supplements of these nutrients without consulting your health care practitioner. Please also consider that many of these nutrients can be obtained from your diet.

Vitamin A

The functions of vitamins A and D comprise the foundation of our health, regulating genetic activity that causes cells to make proteins required by water-soluble vitamins and minerals. Vitamin A deficiency is rare since common animal and plant foods contain this nutrient. Therefore, vitamin A supplementation is usually unnecessary.

A note of caution—when cod liver oil or retinol supplements such as retinyl acetate and retinyl palmitate are consumed on a regular basis, vitamin A toxicity may occur. Excess vitamin A in the body causes havoc because it prevents vitamin D from influencing the genetic activity described above. Vitamin A supplementation may obviate the wonderful benefits of vitamin D. Please be careful!

Vitamin K2

Vitamins K2 and D partner to build and maintain strong bones and teeth as well as fight cardiovascular disease. Vitamin D's functions include regulating calcium absorption in the intestines to maintain bones and dental health. However, once calcium enters the blood stream, vitamin D relinquishes control of the mineral's destination to a less-known nutrient called vitamin K2—one of the Vitamin D Wellness Protocol trio—that moves calcium out of the arteries and into the bones and teeth.

Let's take a look at vitamin K2 and how it complements vitamin D. Like vitamins A and D, vitamin K belongs to a family of fat-soluble nutrients. Two distinct forms of vitamin K offer medical value: phylloquinone and menaquinone.

Phylloquinone, or vitamin K1, is present in all green plants that acquire energy from sunlight. Green leafy vegetables including spinach, kale, collard greens, broccoli, and Brussels sprouts abound with vitamin K1. Clotting blood is primarily vitamin K1's life-saving benefit. Vitamin K1 constantly recycles in the body, so deficiency is rare.

Menaquinone, or vitamin K2, differs greatly from K1. First, there are two forms of vitamin K2: menaquinone-4 (MK-4) found in *grass-fed* animal protein including meat, egg yolk, butter, some cheeses, and calf's liver. A more potent form of menaquinone, called vitamin K2 (MK-7), is abundant in a fermented soybean called natto.

Health benefits of adequate vitamin K2 levels include potential prevention of osteoporosis, arterial plaque, and dental cavities. Vitamin K2 moves calcium to the bones and teeth, as well as sweeps calcium from soft tissue lining such as the arteries. Specifically, vitamin K2 activates proteins (osteocalcin and MGP (matrix gla protein)), which are produced by vitamin D that facilitate moving calcium to where it belongs: the bones and teeth.

Low vitamin K2 levels, however, are common and may pose health risks. First, vitamin K2 receptors need regular replenishment as they are not recycled in the body. Second, the vitamin's natural sources are lacking in most diets. Owing to the reliance on industrial farming in many parts of the world, many people are low in vitamin K2. When insufficient vitamin K2 is in the blood stream, calcium can linger along arterial pathways potentially causing calcification, the process whereby calcium deposits form plaque accumulating in the cardiovascular system.

Supplementing with adequate vitamin D and K2 balances calcium metabolism. The concept of "balance" is important: one can enjoy optimal vitamin D levels but unknowingly have a vitamin K2 deficiency, a potential recipe for the development of cardiovascular disease. Unless you ingest *grass-fed* animal products or soy-laden natto on a regular basis, consider taking a daily K2 supplement that does not contain soy products. (For example, soy can interfere with thyroid medication.) Some experts recommend a daily dose between 90 and 120 mcg. WARNING: Some anticoagulant medications (blood thinners such as warfarin) block the action of vitamin K. If you are taking any blood thinning medication, please check with your health care professional before adding *any form of vitamin K* to your body.

Calcium

The essential mineral calcium is the best known of vitamin D's partners. Vitamin D regulates calcium's absorption in the intestines so it can contribute to bone and dental health.

Calcium deficiency tends to be uncommon as most Western diets contain sufficient calcium including dairy products, leafy green vegetables, and fish products. Calcium supplementation, however, remains a topic of debate within the medical community. While calcium is essential to the bones and teeth, this mineral can linger throughout the body, potentially causing calcification in soft tissue including the kidneys and cardiovascular system.

If you are taking a calcium supplement, you may want to reconsider. Since understanding the danger of calcification of soft tissues, I have not taken a calcium supplement because my serum calcium level is within normal range. Furthermore, I consume a daily vitamin K2 supplement to increase the likelihood that the calcium in my body is moved from the bloodstream to my bones and teeth.

Magnesium

The mineral magnesium is a member of the Vitamin D Wellness Protocol trio, which includes vitamins D3 and K2. In particular, magnesium is essential to vitamin D's metabolism and absorption. An abundance of medical literature indicates that magnesium is one of the most important elements in maintaining good health. Its benefits include energy production, protection of the nervous system, improvement of muscle function, and a decrease in cardiovascular disease risk. Low magnesium levels may impair the conversion of circulating vitamin D to the activated form, denying your body vitamin D's amazing health benefits.

In today's world of fast food and pharmaceutical drugs, magnesium deficiency is common.

Many diets lack natural sources of magnesium including green leafy vegetables, legumes, seeds, and nuts. Furthermore, prolific use of prescription drugs including antibiotics, proton pump inhibitors, and osteoporosis medications contributes to depletion of the body's magnesium levels. A daily magnesium supplement of at least 400 mg may boost your levels of this important mineral.

Phosphorus

Phosphorus (phosphate) is a mineral that interacts with activated vitamin D and parathyroid hormones to help maintain the balance of calcium. A wide variety of foods such as beef, chicken, eggs, seafood, legumes, nuts, grains, and dairy products contain ample amounts of phosphorus. Phosphorus imbalance is rare except for persons with excess or extremely low blood calcium or kidney disorders. Unless encouraged by a health care practitioner, phosphorus supplementation is not recommended.

Zinc

The essential mineral zinc works with activated vitamin D to bolster the immune system and influences healthy cell function. Zinc is commonly found in shellfish, red meats, beans, poultry, and nuts. Although zinc deficiency is rare, some people choose to supplement with it, about 50 mg per day.

Boron

The trace mineral boron is essential to activated vitamin D's metabolism as well as the breakdown of calcium and magnesium. Boron is contained in fruits, vegetables, seeds, nuts, and other foods produced in plants. Deficiency of boron is rare as its sources are common in most diets. Some people choose to supplement boron but for most persons it is unnecessary.

Concluding Thoughts

Vitamin D functions in concert with fat-soluble vitamins A and K2 as well as several minerals. To reap the health benefits of vitamin D, you should be aware of its biochemical partners, specifically vitamin K2 and magnesium, which are included in the Vitamin D Wellness Protocol. The next chapter addresses how to test each vitamin D partner as well as your parathyroid hormone.

4

LABORATORY TESTING

Testing your vitamin D level is paramount to achieving and maintaining safe optimal status. In addition, testing specific vitamin D partners or related biochemicals may be a good idea depending on your individual situation. Remember that vitamin D and its cofactors must be *balanced* to be effective.

Except where noted, the words "testing" and "test" mean blood is collected in your medical professional's office, local laboratory, or at home, and fasting prior to the test is not required unless noted in this chapter. Reference ranges of biochemicals vary from laboratory to laboratory so please use the numbers here only as a general guide. As always, I recommend undergoing testing under the care of your health care professional.

Vitamin D

Your first vitamin D test establishes your vitamin D baseline. The gold standard test for vitamin D is called **25(OH)D** or 25-hydroxyvitamin D where your available, or circulating, vitamin D (calcidiol) in the bloodstream is measured. The optimal range is equal to, or greater than, 100 ng/mL (250 nmol/L).

Another vitamin D test is called 1,25(OH)2D or 1,25-dihydroxyvitamin D where your activated vitamin D (calcitriol) is measured. This test is *not* the preferred test by vitamin D experts for these reasons: a) the biological half-life of calcitriol is shorter than calcidiol and b) the test is less accurate because the 1,25(OH)2D is influenced by the parathyroid hormone (PTH) as well as other hormones. Ensure the 25(OH)D, *not* the 1,25(OH)2D, test is ordered.

Calcium

Calcium is absorbed in the intestines through the action of vitamin D. A more-than-optimal vitamin D level may cause too much calcium in soft tissues and organs. So, it would be a good idea to test your serum calcium, which measures the total calcium in your blood. If **serum calcium** level is more than 10.9 mg/dL, then your parathyroid hormone should be tested.

Ionized calcium is the free, most active form of calcium. You must fast for the ionized calcium test, which should be taken if excess calcium or PTH is a suspected issue. The normal rage of ionized calcium is a level between 4.64 and 5.28 mg/dL. Low ionized calcium may indicate, *inter alia*, a vitamin D deficiency and/or low parathyroid hormone (hypoparathyroidism); abnormally high ionized calcium may suggest excess calcium and/or an overactive parathyroid gland (hyperparathyroidism).

Another method to ascertain calcium status, including the amount of calcification of the arteries, is to undergo a CT (pronounced "cat") scan for your cardiac calcium. The name of the test is "**CT coronary artery calcium (CAC)" scoring**. Valid for up to five years and unknown to most of the public, the CAC test is easy, fast, and non-invasive, and can be scheduled at your local radiology diagnostics center. The amount of radiation exposure is about equivalent to a mammogram, and no contrast dye is required.

The encouraging news is that the American Heart Association recommended the **CAC** test in its November 2018 cholesterol guidelines for determining cardiac calcium risk status and the need for statins for people aged 40 to 75 years. At the time of this writing, however, many health insurance plans do not cover the cost of this test. In my opinion, the test fee (usually less than US$200) is well worth the money. This test may save your, or a loved one's, life!

Vitamin K2

Vitamin K2 partners with vitamin D to move calcium out of the blood stream, soft tissues, and organs and into the bones and teeth. There is no generally available test to measure directly forms of vitamin K. However, a CAC test may provide insight into the effectiveness of vitamin K2 intake in your cardiovascular system. In other words, if your CAC score, serum calcium, and/or ionized calcium are low, your consumption of vitamin K2 probably is effective. If your CAC score, serum calcium, and/or ionized calcium are high, then your parathyroid hormone should be tested.

Parathyroid Hormone

Nestled behind the thyroid gland, four tiny parathyroid glands in your neck play an important role in your body: they regulate calcium. When calcium levels are too low, the glands release **parathyroid hormone (PTH)** to restore the calcium to its normal range. Conversely, when calcium levels rise, the parathyroid glands stop releasing PTH, potentially causing a range of symptoms including kidney stones and bone pain.

Three forms of PTH are assayed in this test for which *fasting is required*. The reference ranges are: N-terminal: 8 to 24 pg/mL; C-terminal: 50 to 330 pg/mL; and intact molecule: 10 to 65 pg/mL. If any of your PTH forms are out-of-range, then explore further options with your doctor. For example, high PTH (hyperparathyroidism) could be directly related to a low vitamin D status.

Magnesium

The mineral magnesium plays an important role in absorption of vitamin D and calcium. The two most common magnesium tests are called serum magnesium and RBC magnesium. **Serum magnesium** is often ordered by health care professionals and evaluates the amount of magnesium in the bloodstream. The "normal" optimal range for the serum magnesium test is 1.7 to 2.2 mg/dL.

The **RBC magnesium** test however is preferred, owing to its accuracy. Most of the magnesium in the body is absorbed in the cells; this test measures the magnesium in the RBC or "red blood cells." According to Dr. Carolyn Dean, a renowned magnesium expert, the optimal range of the RBC magnesium test is 6.0 to 6.5 mg/dL.

Phosphorus

Absorbed in the intestines, the mineral phosphorus interacts with vitamin D, calcium, and PTH. The **serum phosphorus/phosphate** test measures the amount of inorganic phosphate in the blood; urine testing also is available. Phosphorus deficiencies are associated, *inter alia*, with malabsorption, excess calcium, uncontrolled diabetes, and kidney disorders. The "normal" reference range for serum phosphorus/phosphate is 2.8 to 4.5 mg/dL.

Zinc

A cofactor of vitamin D, the mineral *zinc* can be measured by taking a plasma (not serum) blood test called "**zinc**." (Zinc is challenging to detect in blood serum as it is only distributed in trace amounts to the cells.) Zinc also can be tested using a urine test or hair analysis. Zinc deficiency affects approximately two billion people across the globe. Low zinc is associated, *inter alia*, with gut health issues, autism, and mental health challenges. The "normal" reference range for the plasma zinc test is 10.0 to 17.0 μmol/L.

Boron

Boron is a little-known element that is one of vitamin D's partners. While it is not typical to supplement with **boron**, some people do, and testing may be in order. A "normal" reference range is fewer than 50 μg/L.

Vitamin A

Fasting is required for the **vitamin A** test that measures retinol, the animal form of vitamin A. Deficiency in vitamin A is rare in the developed world. Nonetheless, a low level may indicate malabsorption of this vitamin D partner. On the other hand, high vitamin A may suggest, *inter alia*, consumption of excess cod liver oil, which can cause unpleasant symptoms, including liver damage, bone pain, and severe drowsiness. The reference range of vitamin A for adults is 38 to 98 μg/dL.

Concluding Thoughts

Nature's *balance* of vitamin D and its cofactors works in unison. For most people, testing vitamin D—the 25(OH)D test—and serum calcium every six months is adequate to monitor your Vitamin D Wellness levels. In some cases, an out-of-range measurement can lead to more tests. With that said, it is usually unnecessary to run the gamut of the tests addressed in this chapter unless ordered by your doctor. And, as we see, much of the available testing is related to balancing calcium–a vital mineral that commands "a check and balance" to ensure optimal health!

Part II is next—the centerpiece of *Defend Your Life III*—where we learn about vitamin D and immunity with emphasis on vitamin D's role in coronaviruses.

PART II

Vitamin D and Immunity

5

INTRODUCTION TO IMMUNITY

The subtitle of this book is "Vitamin D and Immunity." You have reviewed the basics of vitamin D in the initial part of *Defend Your Life III*. The second part looks at immunity, and to what extent vitamin D positively affects it.

What Is Immunity?

Immunity is a widely used medical term describing the state of the immune system, which is an unseen "largely conceptual entity devoted to protecting us from invisible threats," according to the author of *On Immunity* Eula Biss. In other words, the immune system is not a visible entity like an organ or a gland.

The primary purpose of the immune system is to prevent or limit pathogens such as viruses that can cause contagious illnesses. Simply stated, *pathogens* are germs that can cause disease. Furthermore, when a pathogen is viewed as dangerous to the immune system, it invokes the formation of antibodies called *antigens.*

Immunity Cells

This vital, complex immune system comprises billions of immune cells located in various parts of the body, including the skin, bone marrow, and the bloodstream. Different types of immune cells that circulate in the body include macrophages, neutrophils, and "natural killer" cells such as B- and T-cells.

- *Macrophages* are large white blood cells in healthy tissue that await an attack by pathogens such as viruses and bacteria. When a pathogen emerges, macrophages release proteins called *cytokines* to fight the pathogen.

After the battle ends, macrophages clean up the dead pathogens.

- *Neutrophils* are the front-line, white blood cells that surround and capture pathogens. Since they only live for about a day, *neutrophils* can also signal other white blood cells to attack and destroy foreign pathogens.

- *Lymphocytes,* or "natural killer" white blood cells, include B- and T-cells provide extra lines of defense against pathogens.

    - The B-cell, an adaptive immunity cell, slows down and neutralizes pathogens by producing Y-shaped proteins called antibodies (red antibodies surrounding pathogens are illustrated on the book cover). These antibodies fight infection.

    - *T-cells* target and attack a pathogen. For example, once the T-cell learns the genetic code of a novel pathogen, it trains other T-cells to destroy the infected cells.

Let's look at three types of immunity: innate, adaptive, and passive. In addition, we will address the antithesis of immunity called autoimmunity, the cause of a number of serious diseases.

Innate Immunity

Innate immunity is simply the defense system with which we were born. This system involves barriers that keep some antigens from entering our bodies. In other words, innate immunity is our first line of defense. Examples of innate immunity include mucus, the skin, and the cough reflex.

Adaptive Immunity

Adaptive immunity develops by exposure to various antigens that are new to our bodies. This type of immunity involves white blood cells or sensitized lymphocytes such as T- and B-cells. These cells learn to differentiate between our own body tissues and substances that are foreign to our body. Once the lymphocytes are developed, they will multiply and provide memory for our immune system. Examples of adaptive immunity include the identity and mechanisms of action for contagious illnesses such as reactions to COVID-19, influenza, and the common cold.

When adaptive immunity is suppressed,

cytokines that regulate inflammation are released. This strong adverse reaction to invading pathogens, for example, COVID-19, can result in a *cytokine storm* or an overdrive of the immune system, potentially detrimental to cells at the organ level.

Passive Immunity

Passive immunity occurs when antibodies are made in a body other than our own. A classic example pertains to babies who inherit passive immunity from their mothers.

First, maternal antibodies are passed to the unborn baby through the placenta during the last trimester. The number and types of antibodies passed to the baby depend on the mother's immunity. In addition, immunity in newborn babies is temporary and decreases from the ages of six to twelve months.

Second, breastfeeding can extend a baby's passive immunity. Breast milk contains antibodies from the mother, and the *colostrum* (viscous, yellowish breast milk) is replete with antibodies during the first few days after birth.

Passive immunity also can involve the transfusion of donated *antiserum*, which is prepared by medical personnel to protect against specific diseases. For example, persons who recovered from COVID-19 can donate their antiserum to help other COVID-19 patients overcome the virus.

Autoimmunity

When the adaptive immune system is not strong enough to fight external threats such as infections, it can go awry by signaling antibodies and T-cells to attack healthy cells. This response is called *autoimmunity*—when the body's immune cells attack its own healthy cells. Examples of autoimmune diseases include Type 1 diabetes mellitus, lupus ("systemic lupus erythematosus" or SLE), multiple sclerosis, thyroid diseases such as Hashimoto's, and rheumatoid arthritis. You also can find detailed information on vitamin D and autoimmune diseases in Chapter 11 of the book *Defend Your Life II.*

Concluding Thoughts

Immunity encompasses the whole body's defense of protecting against known and foreign invaders. The immune system is invisible to the naked eye but lies in billions of cells. The main types of immunity are innate, adaptive, and passive. In addition, autoimmunity, the direct opposite of immunity, can cause serious diseases.

In the next several chapters let's look at how vitamin D can "defend your life" by fighting pathogens such as viruses.

6

VITAMIN D'S ROLE IN IMMUNITY

Some years ago, renowned U.S. vitamin D expert Michael F. Holick, PhD, MD, made a bold statement about vitamin D's capability to help protect us from the millions of pathogens that surround us daily. He aptly summarized the role of vitamin D and immunity by stating,

> *"To say vitamin D has anti-inflammatory, antimicrobial, antiviral, anti-anything properties is*

an understatement. Vitamin D may be one of our most reliable proactive ingredients in bolstering comprehensive immunity and reinforcing the body's natural defenses."

Scientific research over the past several decades solidifies the connection between vitamin D levels and immunity. Vitamin D plays an integral part in the regulation of the immune system. Adequate vitamin D in our bodies can protect us from invading pathogens because the immune cells contain vitamin D receptors (VDR). (You can find an explanation of VDR in Chapter 1).

Attached to the surface of the immune cells, VDR act as "gate keepers" by signaling when invader pathogens are trying to invade a healthy cell. The VDR must be replete with activated vitamin D to effectively regulate immunity cells. When the VDR attached to immune cells do not contain sufficient vitamin D to attack invaders, they enable pathogens to defeat the immune cells. Therefore, diseases and illnesses can develop.

Let's look at the various types of immunity and how they are affected by vitamin D levels.

Vitamin D Affects Babies' Innate Immune System

The vitamin D status of expectant mothers can affect the vitamin D in a fetus. The vitamin D health of the mother's placenta influences the baby's innate immunity. A robust innate immunity may lead to a stronger adaptive immunity that can fight pathogens that are novel to the child.

- Researchers from Canada's McGill University conducted a review of vitamin D's role in innate immunity. They described vitamin D as a "key regulator of innate responses to [a] microbial threat." Production of activated vitamin D at infected areas promotes front-line innate immune responses. This important review of vitamin D's mechanism of action regarding the innate immune system was published in the July 2021 issue of the journal *Reviews in Endocrine and Metabolic Disorders*.

Vitamin D Helps to Regulate the Adaptive Immune System

Scientific research over the past three decades solidifies the connection between vitamin D and adaptive immunity. VDR attach to the surface of the adaptive immune system's antibodies and sensitized lymphocytes. However, the VDR must be replete with vitamin D to effectively regulate adaptive immunity. When the VDR receive adequate amounts of vitamin D, they enable the adaptive immune system to function properly by attacking new and previous invaders.

- The best examples of vitamin D's role include 2020 and 2021 research that was conducted to learn about the association of vitamin D status and how vitamin D levels positively adapt to the onset of COVID-19. Overall, studies indicate that people with higher vitamin D levels have a lower risk of contracting the highly contagious disease that has seized the planet.

Vitamin D Affects the Passive Immune System

The direct correlation between the content of a mother's milk and her vitamin D status affects the baby's passive immune system. Unless a lactating mother enjoys adequate vitamin D during pregnancy, vitamin D deficiency results in less vitamin D for the baby during lactation.

- Published in late 2020, a study by researchers Carol L. Wagner, MD and Bruce W. Hollis, PhD of the Medical University of South Carolina focused on the effects of vitamin D on pregnancy and lactation. They concluded, *inter alia*, that when a mother is deficient in vitamin D, her milk does not contain enough vitamin D for the baby. Drs. Wagner and Hollis recommended a daily vitamin D supplementation dose of 6,400 IU for the lactating mom.

Part II of the book *Defend Your Life II* addresses in detail how vitamin D status may passively affect children's health from preconception to the neonatal period.

Vitamin D and Autoimmunity

The antithesis of adaptive immunity is autoimmunity. When the VDR attached to the adaptive immune system's cells do not contain adequate vitamin D to attack invaders, autoimmunity may kick in, causing the death of healthy immune cells. Thus, low vitamin D levels may lead to the development of autoimmune diseases including multiple sclerosis, rheumatoid arthritis, and lupus.

Multiple Sclerosis (MS)

Multiple sclerosis (MS) befits a disease of modern civilization, one of sun avoidance. Initially identified by French neurologist Jean-Martin Charcot in 1868, MS is a chronic, neurological autoimmune disorder that damages the myelin sheath, the multiple layers of fatty tissue that surround and protect, *inter alia,* the nerves in the brain, spinal cord, and eyes. When the myelin sheath is intact, electrical impulses are carried through the nerves with accuracy and speed. When the myelin sheath is damaged ("sclerosis" is the scar tissue formed by damaged myelin), the nerves do not conduct electrical impulses normally. The impulses are distorted or interrupted, resulting in a range of symptoms including numbness, blindness, paralysis, and brain damage. MS also can result in death.

Despite the identification of MS more than one-hundred-fifty years ago, MS has no cure. Over 2.8 million people around the world have been diagnosed with MS including about one million Americans. Women are two to three times more likely to develop MS than men. Although MS is usually diagnosed between the ages of 20 and 50, the disease can strike at any age. In addition, Caucasian women of northern European descent are more frequently diagnosed with MS than African Americans, Hispanics, and Asians.

- A team of researchers from India and the United States conducted an in-depth review of the science associated with vitamin D and MS. The scientists found that there is "a strong correlation" between low vitamin D and the development and progression of MS. The team recommended "vitamin D supplementation be incorporated in current treatment protocols for MS."

The great news is that the results of vitamin D research are in practice! Dr. Cicero Galli Coimbra, a neurologist practicing in Sao Paulo, Brazil, has successfully treated MS patients with daily, high-dose (40,000 to 200,000 IU) vitamin D. His Coimbra Protocol has successfully treated MS patients to the point where they are in complete remission!

> *"For a healthy person, I can say without a doubt that 10,000 IU of vitamin D a day will not pose any risk, quite the contrary. For those who suffer from any autoimmune disease, this dose will bring partial relief, but will not eliminate the problem. Higher doses can be used, provided this supplementation is done under medical supervision."*
>
> ~ *Dr. Cicero Coimbra*

Practice of the Coimbra Protocol has expanded beyond Brazil to other South American countries, Europe, and North America. For more information about the Coimbra Protocol, its doctors, and patients, please see my recommendations in the "Additional Resources" section in the back of this book.

Rheumatoid Arthritis (RA)

About one percent of the global population suffers from rheumatoid arthritis (RA). One to two million Americans suffer from RA. Most RA victims are women, but men also develop the disease. Although the debilitating illness can occur at any age, RA usually strikes persons between the ages of 25 and 50.

Rheumatoid arthritis (RA) is an autoimmune disease that causes pain, swelling, and stiffness in the joints, mainly affecting the wrists, elbows, fingers, knees, ankles, toes, and neck. In RA patients the immune system attacks the joint lining, causing inflammation, usually striking both sides of the body at about the same time, resulting in severely impaired mobility in the upper or lower body.

Unlike the more common osteoarthritis, RA also can adversely affect the body's organ systems including the heart, lungs, kidneys, and nerves. Complications of RA can eventually destroy the joints as well as cause lung disease, heart failure, neuropathy, anemia, eye disease, or inflammation of the blood vessels.

- A 2021 case-control study was conducted at a tertiary (specialized) care hospital. The research focused on the connection between

> vitamin D status and rheumatoid arthritis. Six hundred patients, half of whom received a recent diagnosis of RA, and the remaining half comprising the control group, were enrolled in the study. The researchers found a "prevalence of vitamin D deficiency in patients with RA, and there is a link with disease severity." The team also concluded that vitamin D supplementation may be needed to prevent or treat RA.

SLE (Lupus)

Lupus ("systemic lupus erythematosus" or SLE) is a chronic autoimmune disease that attacks the body's healthy cells, tissues, and organs. This disease results in severe inflammation, fatigue, and, in some cases, death.

About 1.5 million Americans, and at least five million persons globally, suffer from a form of lupus, according to the Lupus Foundation of America. Ninety percent of persons diagnosed with lupus are women, many of whom are in their reproductive years.

Research suggests that adequate vitamin D in the body may protect against the development of SLE. Genetic and environmental factors as well as vitamin D deficiency have been linked to lupus.

Sensitivity to sunlight, the primary source of vitamin D, is common among SLE patients.

Scientific research indicates a high prevalence of vitamin D deficiency among those persons suffering lupus.

- Spanish researchers conducted a cross-sectional study of 264 patients, most of whom being female, to understand better the effect of low vitamin D on lupus patients. The research team concluded that a high prevalence of low vitamin D existed in Caucasian SLE patients who not only experienced disease activity but endured damage from the disease.

Concluding Thoughts

Adequate vitamin D status plays an important role in strengthening innate, adaptive, and passive immunity systems. In addition, insufficient vitamin D status may contribute the development of autoimmunity. Conversely, adequate vitamin D can prevent and treat some types of autoimmune diseases. Vitamin D supplementation is so effective in treating MS that the Coimbra Protocol has gained widespread success.

Upcoming chapters in this second part of the

book address the science behind the findings of vitamin D's effects on the prevention and treatment of contagious respiratory viruses including COVID-19, influenza, RSV, and the common cold.

7

CORONAVIRUSES

Emerging from Wuhan, China in late 2019, a novel coronavirus took the world by storm, causing millions of deaths, wreaking global economic havoc, and instilling widespread anxiety and fear. The highly contagious, respiratory coronavirus, identified as COVID-19, quickly developed into a pandemic in early 2020. At the time of this writing during winter 2022, the deadly virus and its variants continue to rage across the planet.

What Are Coronaviruses?

Coronaviruses are identified by their crown-shaped ("corona" is the Spanish word for "crown") spikes on the spherical surface of the virus. The spikes enter human cells, potentially causing a coronavirus. However, these unique spikes are readily recognized by the immune system. The effectiveness of the immune system depends upon the strength of its defense.

Severe acute respiratory syndrome (SARS-CoV) and Middle East respiratory syndrome (MERS-CoV) are examples of human coronaviruses. The global outbreak of SARS-CoV peaked in 2003.

Transmitted by duodenal camels to humans, MERS-CoV was identified in 2012 with outbreaks in some Arab Peninsula countries, as well as the Republic of Korea.

It is interesting to note about 20 percent of the common cold incidences are coronaviruses.

SARS-CoV-2 is the medical acronym used to label COVID-19. However, this chapter characterizes the virus as "COVID-19."

SUE'S STORY: Enroute from the United States to Cambodia on December 7, 2019, my travel companion and I connected to a flight in Guangzhou, China. At that time, Chinese authorities had not released information about a deadly viral outbreak in their country. When walking through the Guangzhou airport, I noticed a woman quietly observing transiting passengers. Seconds after noting this, all transiting passengers were required to enter an apparent screening area with turnstiles. I observed a male scanning thermal images of passengers going through the screening equipment. I opined to my traveling friend, "There's something going on here. Could be some type of a health outbreak." Returning to the Guangzhou airport a week later, we experienced similar screening procedures.

Over a month later, the Chinese government released information about the coronavirus outbreak in Wuhan to the rest of the world. Our lifestyles soon changed. More importantly, the numbers of COVID-19 cases, hospitalizations, and deaths continue. The rest is heart-wrenching history. The deaths caused by COVID-19 surpassed the number of fatalities from the infamous 1918-1919 Spanish influenza pandemic.

COVID-19 is mainly transmitted from one person to another via respiratory droplets from coughing, sneezing, or merely talking or laughing. Public health organizations emphasized the need to mitigate the virus spread. Preventative measures included wearing face coverings, practicing social distancing, and frequently washing hands.

But what about vitamin D supplementation? Understanding vitamin D's role in immunity, we look at the vitamin's possible contribution in preventing and treating COVID-19.

First, we look at the association between vitamin D deficiency and COVID-19. Second, we focus on recent medical literature about adequate vitamin D status and how it may prevent or treat COVID-19.

NOTE: Please understand that vitamin D adequacy neither encompasses the entire solution to avoiding the development of COVID-19 nor acts as a treatment for this virus.

What is the Association between Vitamin D Deficiency and COVID-19?

Medical research has studied the vulnerability of people with vitamin D deficiency (less than 20 ng/mL or 45 nmol/L)* and their likelihood of developing COVID-19. (*Please note that the global scientific communities have yet to agree how to characterize the range of vitamin D measurements. The value stated here is based on dated the Endocrine Society guidelines.)

- A 2021 study by University of Florida researchers found that COVID-19 patients with vitamin D deficiency were 4.6 times more likely to test positive for the illness than patients without vitamin D deficiency. Furthermore, vitamin D-deficient patients were five times more likely to be infected with COVID-19 than patients with vitamin D sufficiency.

- Russian researchers teamed with Dr. William B. Grant of the United States to examine the relationship between low vitamin D status and severity and death among 133 hospitalized COVID-19 patients. They concluded that "severe vitamin D deficiency is associated with increased risk of COVID-19 severity and fatal outcome." Severe vitamin D deficiency is characterized by these researchers as 10 ng/mL (25 nmol/L).

- International researchers collaborated on a literature review to understand better the connection between vitamin D status and COVID-19 patients. They concluded that low vitamin D levels are associated with greater incidence and poor outcomes of COVID-19 patients. This 2021 study was published in the *European Journal of Medical and Health Sciences.*

- A team of German scientists explored whether low vitamin D is causal or if vitamin D deficiency negatively affects the immune system. By performing a systematic review and meta-analysis of research, including clinical studies, on the association of vitamin D and COVID-19, the researchers found "strong evidence" that low vitamin D is a "predictor rather than just a side effect of the infection." Their study was published in the journal *Nutrients* in October 2021.

- Finally, a Canadian researcher, Dr. Rbab Taha, teamed with Saudi Arabian scientists to assess vitamin D's role in preventing and healing COVID-19. They characterized vitamin D supplementation as a possible "hope." The research team added that one should avoid vitamin D deficiency to strengthen the immune system and its protective effect during COVID-19.

The last study addressed in this section offers a good segue into vitamin D supplementation's possible role in protective against and treating COVID-19.

Could Vitamin D Prevent COVID-19?

At the time of this writing, few medical studies about vitamin D's role in preventing COVID-19 have been published. However, I cite this study as well as offer an anecdotal personal story about possible prevention.

- Published in the *World Journal of Virology*, a study conducted by Greek researchers and U.S. vitamin D expert Dr. Michael F. Holick aimed to clarify the role of vitamin D supplementation in European countries during the COVID-19 pandemic. They concluded that people having a vitamin D level of 40-60 ng/mL (100-150 nmol/L) may be protected from "serious-critical illness" or death from COVID-19.

SUE'S STORY: During the pandemic, I took 20,000 IU daily to bolster my immune system. I believe that my consistent optimal vitamin D level (over 100 ng/mL (250 nmol/L)) played a role in protecting me from developing COVID-19.

First, remember my previous story about apparent passive and active screening for COVID-19 at an airport in China? Thankfully, I did not develop COVID-19 from transiting through the airport with hundreds of passengers, some of whom might have been carrying this highly contagious disease.

Second, in August 2020, my husband contracted COVID-19. He tested positive, and I—negative. Thankfully, he recovered (with steroidal treatment) in less than two weeks and was not hospitalized. Meanwhile, we lived together during this trying time. Throughout, and after, my husband's bout with COVID-19, I tested negative. I credit my optimal vitamin D level (more than 100 ng/mL or 250 nmol/L) as protective against contracting COVID-19, but this "evidence" is only anecdotal.

Could Vitamin D Treat COVID-19?

Medical research indicates that there *is* a relationship between vitamin D treatment and improved outcomes in COVID-19 patients:

- Published in the 2022 January issue of the journal *Bone*, a U.S. study examined the effectiveness of administering calcitriol (Chapter 1) to hospitalized COVID-19 patients. The randomized pilot study enrolled fifty patients, twenty-five of whom received 0.5 μg of activated vitamin D3 (a small dose of calcitriol) for fourteen days. (The twenty-five control patients received no calcitriol treatment.) The researchers concluded that patients who received calcitriol benefited from oxygen (not ventilation) treatment.

- Slovakian researchers sought to determine the effect of vitamin D supplementation on survival of 207 COVID-19 patients. Thirty-seven patients who had vitamin D levels of less than 20 ng/mL (50 nmol/L) or between 21 and 30 ng/mL (52.5 to 75 nmol/L) received a single dose of 300,000 IU of vitamin D. The remaining one hundred-seventy individuals did not receive vitamin D supplementation. One patient who received the large vitamin D amount died. Twenty-four patients without the vitamin D supplementation however perished. The scientists concluded that a single 300,000 IU dose of vitamin D appears to represent "a useful, practical, and safe adjunctive approach for the treatment and prevention of COVID-19." (NOTE: If you would like to take more than 10,000 IU of vitamin D daily, consult your healthcare provider before doing so. A single dose of 300,000 IU is experimental and should not be construed as a "normal" dose.)

- An international team of researchers conducted a medical literature review to determine the link between vitamin D status and the severity of COVID-19 patients. The researchers concluded that the therapeutic use of vitamin D is advantageous in the management of COVID-19.

- Led by Dr. Gaelle Annweiler of the University of Angers, a largely French team performed research on seventy-seven elderly persons whose average age was eighty-eight and who were hospitalized for COVID-19. The researchers determined that in the elderly "vitamin D supplementation was associated with less severe COVID-19 and better survival."

- An American team's findings correlate with the largely French study (above) about the positive treatment and increased recovery of patients with COVID-19. The Americans emphasized returning to the basics and surmised that discontinuing vitamin D supplementation may increase the mortality and morbidity in COVID-19 patients. Furthermore, achieving and maintaining adequate vitamin D status may assist in treating COVID-19 patients as well as "potentially decrease recovery time and improve outcome."

Concluding Thoughts

The scientific evidence, at the time of this writing, indicates the vital role that adequate vitamin D supplementation may play in preventing and treating COVID-19. However, large, well-designed, randomized clinical trials are needed to address further the efficacy of vitamin D supplementation to defend against and treat the coronavirus COVID-19.

The next chapter addresses other contagious respiratory illnesses that vitamin D may defend against.

8

OTHER RESPIRATORY VIRUSES

Coronaviruses are not the only respiratory viruses that are highly contagious and sometimes deadly. In this chapter we look at a few primary respiratory viruses: influenza, an illness called RSV, and the common cold.

Before doing so, let's briefly review vitamin D's mechanism of action regarding viruses. Activated vitamin D regulates the antiviral immune response in the respiratory tract. Not only does activated vitamin D act as an effective defense mechanism against respiratory tract infections but it may prevent excessive inflammation and tissue damage.

Vitamin D and Influenza

According to the World Health Organization (WHO), one *billion* worldwide cases of influenza strike annually. The highly contagious influenza should not be taken lightly. WHO estimates between 290,000 and 650,000 flu-related deaths occur yearly.

- Dr. Rbab Taha, a Canadian researcher, teamed with Saudi Arabian scientists to assess vitamin D's role in preventing and treating respiratory infections including influenza. They performed a review of medical literature of vitamin D's association with influenza. Citing vitamin D's effectiveness in boosting the immune system, the researchers characterized vitamin D as helpful in preventing the onset of influenza. They suggested the need for clinical situations where influenza patients are treated with vitamin D supplementation.

- Led by vitamin D expert Dr. William B. Grant, a team of primarily U.S. advocates looked at evidence of the possibility that vitamin D supplementation may reduce the risk of influenza infections and deaths. They recommended that people, who wish to strengthen their immune system against infections such as influenza, take up to 10,000 IU of vitamin D3 supplements daily to increase their vitamin D level. The team opined that higher vitamin D doses may be helpful for treating influenza but advocated the conduct of randomized controlled and large population studies to evaluate the team's recommendations.

Vitamin D and RSV

Another highly infectious, viral illness is called RSV (respiratory syncytial virus). Although RSV can affect people of all ages, this little-known virus primarily affects infants under the age of one and adults older than 60.

SUE'S STORY: I had not heard of RSV until my elderly Mom contracted it a few years ago. She was super contagious; hospital staff was required to wear full PPE (personal protective equipment) while in her room. After being hospitalized for several weeks, she thankfully recovered.

RSV is the leading cause of hospitalization for infants less than one year old. In fact, RSV in children under one year is sixteen times more likely to cause hospitalization than influenza. If RSV progresses in an individual at any age, the disease can lead to bronchitis or pneumonia.

- A team of researchers from the University of Tokyo investigated the effect of vitamin D on ten Japanese infants under the age of three who suffered from RSV. Eight infants had circulating vitamin D levels of less than 20 ng/mL (50 nmol/L). The results of their study suggested vitamin D deficiency affects the susceptibility to RSV, but not the severity of the disease.

Vitamin D and the Common Cold

Everyone, unfortunately, is familiar with the "common cold." According to the Centers for Disease Control and Prevention, or the CDC, adults average two to three colds annually. Children tend to catch colds more often than adults, averaging six to eight colds per year.

Why is the common cold so common? More than 200 viruses linger in the air and on surfaces and can cause a cold. The types of cold viruses include the "big three": rhinovirus, coronavirus, and RSV. These viruses can lead to other more serious illnesses including bronchitis, pneumonia, and, in some cases, deaths.

- A plethora of pre-2020 published studies confirm that adequate vitamin D may reduce the risk of developing the common cold. Japanese researchers analyzed a randomized, double-blind, placebo-controlled study on vitamin D's effect on the severity of upper respiratory tract infections (URTI). The research team concluded that a "sufficient" (4,000 IU daily for 16 weeks) amount of vitamin D supplementation may treat physical symptoms at the *onset* of a URTI. The researchers added that the quality of life of patients, who are adequately supplementing with vitamin D, may also improve upon the beginning of the infection.

- Published in a 2021 issue of *Brazilian Journal of Otorhinolaryngology*, a study analyzed previous research to evaluate the association of vitamin D and chronic rhinosinusitis, the ongoing inflammation of the sinus and nasal cavities. The scientists concluded that low vitamin D status significantly relates to chronic rhinosinusitis, especially with patients who have nasal polyps.

Concluding Thoughts

Contagious respiratory illnesses can cause havoc with our health. Over the past decade, research has highlighted the association between vitamin D deficiency and the prevention and potentially treatment of, *inter alia*, influenza, RSV, and the common cold. Adequate vitamin D supplementation (at least 10,000 IU daily) may help you avoid development of URTI as well as alleviate symptoms at the onset of these infections.

Furthermore, the economic burden of these illnesses is staggering. For example, in the United

States, the economic loss due to colds alone is about US$25 *billion* per year. Children with colds miss about 22 million days of schooling. Adults forego approximately 22 million days of work. Similar figures tabulate annually!

You may have noticed that the majority of the cited recent (2020 and 2021) research in this chapter pertains to the analysis of previous work. Why? My belief is that the COVID-19 pandemic has affected the publication of new research on non-pandemic-related, medical and scientific research.

On a brighter note, Part III is where we explore how vitamin D status may positively affect aging, cancer, type 2 diabetes, and oral health.

PART III

Vitamin D Prevention and Treatment

9

AGING

Throughout centuries, human beings have sought the out-of-reach "fountain of youth." Achieving adequate vitamin D status however will not culminate in a drink at this fountain. But enjoying an optimal vitamin D level may help you to age more gracefully.

Remember that aging is not only cosmetic but, more importantly, internal. Vitamin D may play a positive role in the condition of your skin as well as other organs, tissues, and cells.

Telomere 101

Prior to addressing recent research on aging, we need to understand the meaning of "telomere." The nucleus of every cell in our body contains forty-six pairs of genetic (DNA) strands called chromosomes. Each chromosome has a "cap" on each end called a telomere. (Think of a shoelace with plastic caps, one at each end of the string.)

Telomeres protect our DNA in the chromosomes. The biological age of our cells is measured by the lengths of our telomeres, which become shorter as we age chronologically and biologically.

The human embryo has the longest telomeres. A newborn baby's telomeres are shorter. Furthermore, a child's telomeres are shorter than an infant's. And so forth.

Telomere length can predict the risk of developing chronic diseases. For example, inflammation is a significant contributor to biological aging as it may shorten telomeres. The shorter the telomere, the faster aging occurs. Conversely, the longer the telomere, the slower aging may transpire.

Latest Research

In this section I address several studies published in 2021 that highlight the positive effects of vitamin D on telomere length. In addition, there is recent research on vitamin D and aging of our largest organ, the skin.

- A largely U.S. study (with a contribution by G. Bocheva from Bulgaria) examined the effect of vitamin D status on skin aging. The researchers found that activated vitamin D (plus a couple precursors) administered orally or topically is promising for preventing and treating premature skin aging.

SUE'S STORY: I am 68 years young, and my skin has its share of wrinkles. However, I have received many compliments about the appearance of my skin including its radiance and smoothness. Perhaps my optimal vitamin D level is at least partially responsible for the condition of my skin.

The centerpiece of my previous vitamin D book *Defend Your Life II* focuses on the importance of adequate vitamin D from preconception through neonatal health. Studies published in 2021 explore how telomere length is affected by maternal vitamin D intake during pregnancy.

- A Belgian study assessed the relationship of maternal vitamin D intake during pregnancy by observing the dietary vitamin D intake of 108 females and examining the telomere length of the pregnant fetus's cord blood. The researchers concluded that vitamin D supplementation specifically during the first trimester is a significant factor associated with telomere length at birth.

- Australian researchers conducted a systematic review of seven studies to determine the effect of maternal nutritional status in pregnancy on the telomere length of the offspring. During pregnancy, the offspring's telomere length was measured in blood, serum, etc. The research team suggested that higher circulating vitamin D (25(OH) D) concentrations in the pregnant women were associated with longer offspring telomere length.

Here is a 2021 study on vitamin D and anti-aging:

- A research team from the Tehran University of Medical Sciences performed a comprehensive review of the association between vitamin D and telomere length. The researchers found that higher vitamin D concentrations are connected to longer telomeres.

- Furthermore, the Iranian team surmised that patients with SLE (systematic lupus erythematosus), the most common form of lupus, an autoimmune disease, may benefit from higher circulating vitamin D levels. Increased vitamin D supplementation may help maintain "telomere length and preventing cellular aging."

Concluding Thoughts

When I published a chapter called "Genetic Aging" in my initial vitamin D book *Defend Your Life*, I was surprised that the subject gained little attention. While my words were not "rocket science," they conveyed the importance of vitamin D supplementation on aging, an association that was, and is, not widely distributed to the general population.

Almost a decade later, research, published in 2021, only accentuates the role vitamin D has as a contributor to anti-aging. In other words, we can help our own aging process by ensuring that we have optimal vitamin D status that offers anti-inflammatory and anti-cancer mechanisms of action.

The next chapter addresses vitamin D and a few cancers: breast, colorectal, pancreatic.

10

CANCER

Cancer remains deadly, despite the billions of dollars that continue to pour into cancer research. According to the International Agency for Research on Cancer, an estimated 18.1 million new cancer cases (excluding nonmelanoma skin cancer) and nearly ten million cancer deaths took place globally in 2020! In fact, cancer is not only a leading cause of death worldwide, but the number of incidences is growing.

Recent research on the association between vitamin D and some cancers gives hope that people with optimal vitamin D status are less likely to develop cancer.

- Esteemed American vitamin D researcher William B. Grant, PhD. conducted a review of vitamin D and cancer. He examined recent research on UVB sunlight, vitamin D levels, vitamin D supplementation, and vitamin D genetics to understand better how vitamin D affects new cancer cases and deaths. Dr. Grant concluded that "vitamin D reduces the risk of cancer incidence and death." His study was published in the January 2020 issue of the journal *Anticancer Research*.

In this chapter we look at recent vitamin D research on three potentially deadly forms of cancer: breast, colorectal, and pancreatic.

Breast Cancer

Over decades, billions of dollars have been devoted to breast cancer research yet little benefit in prevention and treatment has come to fruition.

Breast cancer has surpassed lung cancer as the leading number of global cases in women. In 2020, breast cancer incidence increased by 11.7 percent. Furthermore, breast cancer deaths rose by 6.9 percent!

- A Canadian oncologist performed a systematic review and analysis of twenty-five studies that reported the circulating vitamin D levels in women who were recently diagnosed with breast cancer. Dr. Ioannis Voutsadakis concluded that newly diagnosed breast cancer patients had a high prevalence of low circulating vitamin D. He also stated that the findings "may be linked pathophysiologically with breast cancer development or progression." In addition, Dr. Voutsadakis surmised that vitamin D or its analogues may be useful as a treatment.

- An American research team conducted a review of twenty-two observational studies. On the one hand, the researchers found that low vitamin D is directly related to a greater occurrence of breast cancer. On the other hand, high vitamin D status combined with vitamin D supplementation decreased the incidence of breast cancer.

Colorectal Cancer

Colorectal, or colon, cancer has gained a lot of attention over the past couple decades. Public health campaigns have encouraged regular colonoscopies as an effective screening tool.

Globally, colorectal cancer ranks second in mortality and third in number of cancer incidences. In 2020, the number of colon cancer incidences was up by six percent. And colon cancer deaths increased by 5.8 percent.

- A team of Chinese researchers conducted a systematic review and meta-analysis of the medical literature to explore the relationship of vitamin D and the incidence and prognosis of colorectal cancer. The team's review found that vitamin D status and supplementation decrease the number of incidences. Furthermore, vitamin D may improve the long-term survival of colorectal cancer patients.

Pancreatic Cancer

Pancreatic cancer is the third-leading cause of death in the United States and its incidences are rising. Late diagnosis, early metastasis, and resistance to therapies contribute to this lethal disease.

- Nonetheless, a 2021 U.S. study published in the journal *Cancers* offers some promise. American researchers critically reviewed the science to explore vitamin D regarding the risk, incidence, patient survival, and mortality of pancreatic cancer. Their detailed analysis of numerous research studies including clinical trials indicates that vitamin D shows promise in decreasing the risk and lengthening survival. However, the research team lamented the lack of published, randomized clinical trials (RCTs) that involve vitamin D treatment and pancreatic cancer. The U.S. researchers expressed hope that vitamin D supplementation as well as UVB sunlight exposure offer at least an augmentation of conventional cancer therapies used in pancreatic cancer patients.

I close this section on vitamin D and pancreatic cancer by saying that vitamin D-related genetics do play a role in one's risk of developing pancreatic cancer. For example, single nucleotide polymorphisms, or SNPs, related directly to vitamin D genes (VDR and CYP24A1) are indicators of risk and survival of pancreatic cancer. I remain hopeful about vitamin D's positive role once the findings of additional RCTs are published.

Concluding Thoughts

Staggering statistics of cancer mortality and morbidity continue to grow across our planet. It just boggles my mind that, so few people apparently pay little attention to the benefits of vitamin D supplementation and moderate UVB sunlight.

You may recall from reading Chapter 1 vitamin D's anti-cancer mechanisms of action. These functions are real and do affect cancer manifestations. Activated vitamin D, through its receptors (VDR), regulates cell differentiation, proliferation, and apoptosis (natural cell death). In other words, adequate vitamin D possesses cancer-fighting capabilities!

I remain perplexed why extensive, decades-long cancer research has only minimally impacted positive outcomes. I implore you to consider following the Vitamin D Wellness Protocol that is addressed after Part III. Your health will thank you!

11

DIABETES (TYPE 2)

The number of people with diabetes has soared over the past several decades. According to the World Health Organization and other sources, over 460 million people worldwide have developed Type 2 diabetes mellitus (T2DM). This statistic represents more than six percent of the world's population. Over one million deaths occur globally.

More than 95 percent of diabetics are considered to have T2DM. This lifestyle-induced disease, caused by an "unhealthy" diet and a sedentary existence, involves over-production of blood sugar and the hormone insulin.

Here's what happens as we ingest foods and beverages that trigger high blood sugar: the carbohydrates in our diet are broken down into glucose, which enters the bloodstream. When the beta islet cells in the pancreas detect heightened blood sugar, they secrete insulin.

What is Type 1 Diabetes?

The opposite of T2DM is Type 1 diabetes mellitus (T1DM), a chronic autoimmune disease where the pancreas is unable to produce insulin in its beta islet cells. In the case of T1DM, the body attacks the beta islet cells so they no longer produce insulin.

Affecting about five per cent of diabetics, T1DM usually occurs during childhood or adolescence but can strike at any age. Once T1DM has developed, it never goes away, causing daily monitoring of blood sugar and treatment with insulin intake.

Vitamin D supplementation may play a role in preventing T1DM as the pancreatic beta cells contain vitamin D receptors (VDR). Adequate vitamin D activates the VDR in the beta islet cells, protecting these cells from cytokines, proteins that can destroy beta islet cells.

Insulin helps cells acquire blood glucose and temporarily store it in the liver and muscles as glycogen, the stored form of glucose. After glycogen storage is full, its excess is transformed into, and stored as, fat. If hyperglycemia, or high blood sugar, is untreated, it can lead to the development of T2DM as well as premature deaths ranging from cardiovascular disease to kidney failure.

Association of Vitamin D and T2DM

The medical community as well as the media stress a modified life-style behavior to include eating a "healthy" diet, achieving, and maintaining a "normal" body weight, regular physical activity, etc. to treat T2DM. Unfortunately, I have yet to see a public health guideline such as "supplementing daily with vitamin D" to avoid or treat T2DM.

Recent examples of research that indicate vitamin D's role in combating the onset, as well as the treatment of, T2DM include:

- Led by Dr. A. G. Pittas of the Tufts Medical Center in Boston, Massachusetts, a team conducted a comprehensive review of the medical literature entailing both observational studies and three large clinical trials. Published in 2020 in *The Journal of*

Clinical Endocrinology & Metabolism, the study concluded that vitamin D has a role in influencing diabetes risk. Dr. Pittas and his team also surmised that vitamin D supplementation reduces the risk in prediabetics. Moreover, the study ends with, "Even if the risk reduction [of T2DM] with vitamin D supplementation may appear relatively small, when applied in expanding prediabetes population, it can have important health implications."

- Iranian researchers assessed ten published studies that included a total of 34,882 participants to determine vitamin D's role in the prevention of T2DM. Their analysis indicated that there is an association between vitamin D and T2DM. The researchers cautioned, however, the need for future studies of genetic factors such as VDR variants to complete the analysis of vitamin D and its mechanisms for prevention of T2DM. The study was published in the February 2021 issue of the *European Society for Clinical Nutrition and Metabolism*.

- A 2021 largely American study (plus one contributor from Antigua) explored the role of vitamin D and treatment of T2DM by assessing the impact of vitamin D on glucose (blood sugar). Vitamin D helps control hemoglobin A1c, which measures blood sugar levels over a three-month period. The researchers concluded that vitamin D may reduce hemoglobin A1c as well as alleviate diabetic neuropathy and its symptoms.

Concluding Thoughts

Vitamin D supplementation is associated with T2DM prevention and at least some significant treatments of this type of diabetes, in particular hemoglobin A1c. I am encouraged by the recent research that supports this statement but hope that additional randomized clinical trials will further explore the importance of vitamin D regarding T2DM, a disease that continues to increase globally.

The next chapter addresses dental issues, including oral health and vitamin D.

12

ORAL HEALTH

What does vitamin D have to do with oral health? Well, we know that healthy teeth and gums are part of overall good health. Chapter 3 explains that vitamin K2 moves calcium, activated by vitamin D3, to the teeth and bones.

Teeth are an important part of your body, and calcium and phosphorus create the bony structure that comprises tooth enamel. Dentin, formed under the enamel, contains live cells used to protect the blood supply and nerves inside the tooth. And the jawbone, or the alveolar bone, supports your teeth and gums.

Surprising Statistics

Let's look at some sobering statistics about dental health from the World Health Organization (WHO). The WHO estimates that oral diseases affect about 3.5 billion (yes, billion) people worldwide.

The most common global health condition is untreated tooth decay (dental caries) in permanent teeth. In fact, tooth decay is the most common chronic childhood disease.

Another prevalent oral health disease is severe periodontal (gum) disease, potentially leading to tooth loss, which affects nearly ten per cent of the global population.

Additional WHO statistics pertaining to annual incidences of oral (oropharyngeal) cancer are significant: there are over 450,000 new cases worldwide, and nearly 54,000 new cases each year in the United States. About 10,000 Americans succumb annually to this difficult-to-discover cancer.

Furthermore, treating dental issues is expensive and usually not covered by insurance. The encouraging news is that most dental procedures can be prevented by getting at least annual checkups with your dentist, performing daily oral hygiene, and eating a healthy diet. Unfortunately, vitamin D intake usually is not touted as a dental health partner, but it should be.

Association between Vitamin D and Oral Health

Maintaining good dental hygiene and adequate vitamin D status not only helps your teeth and gums but your overall health. Your oral health as well as vitamin D's anti-inflammatory properties influence organs in your body including gut health. In addition, vitamin D deficiency may be linked to oral cancer. Allowing the health of your mouth to deteriorate may cause medical issues that appear to unrelated to your teeth and gums.

- A comprehensive review of vitamin D deficiency and oral health was published in a 2020 issue of the journal *Nutrients*. Led by Drs. Botelho and Machado of Portugal, the study team examined how vitamin D levels may promote good oral health. The researchers also looked at how vitamin D deficiency may impede oral development. They concluded that vitamin D deficiency "is highly implicated with oral diseases and has been linked with a higher risk of tooth defects, caries, periodontitis and oral treatments." The researchers added, "The maintenance of appropriate 25(OH)D levels has shown to be associated with better oral development and health throughout life."

Children and Dental Disease

It is widely known that untreated dental caries in young children's teeth is highly prevalent. Vitamin D deficiency is most likely a deterrent to a healthy mouth. Here is a study that pertains to children who were the age of seven and low in vitamin D levels:

- Published in a 2021 issue of the journal *Nutrients*, a study from researchers in Porto, Portugal assessed the association between low vitamin D levels (less than 30 ng/mL or 75 nmol/L) and the prevalence of tooth decay in the permanent teeth of seven-year-old children. Based on the results of the study, the permanent teeth of seven-year-old children, whose vitamin D levels (25(OH)D) are less than 30 ng/mL, are associated with advanced dental caries.

Periodontitis

Periodontitis means inflammation of the gums that the surround teeth. Without healthy stable gums, teeth would fall out! Let's look at a 2019 study that examines the effect of vitamin D supplementation on gum disease.

- A team of U.S. researchers embarked on a small pilot study of twenty-three patients who had moderate to severe periodontitis. The patients were randomly assigned to the vitamin D supplementation group or a placebo group. Both groups received a single "intensive" visit that involved scaling and root planning, i.e., deep cleaning, to invoke an inflammatory response. The researchers found that the vitamin D group almost doubled its 25(OH)D levels. In addition, vitamin D supplementation reduced pro-inflammatory salivary cytokines (remember cytokines from Chapter 5?). The research team concluded that vitamin D supplementation may reduce systemic inflammation as well as promote the production of autophagy-related proteins that are connected to anti-microbial functions.

Oral Cancer

Over the past decade the incidences of oral cancer have increased, according to the Oral Cancer Foundation. Oral cancer is one of the most common cancers, yet it usually leads to a poor prognosis as it is challenging to diagnose.

- Researchers from Iran reviewed medical literature for vitamin D's role in oral cancer. Citing the pro-apoptotic, anti-inflammatory, anti-proliferative, anti-invasion, and anti-metastatic mechanisms of action on cancer cells, the team concluded that activated vitamin D (calcitriol) may offer effective treatment on tumor cell death of cutaneous squamous cell carcinoma. The researchers however emphasized the need for further investigation to evaluate vitamin D and its pathways on the development of oral cancer.

Concluding Thoughts

Poor oral health is largely preventable. Adequate vitamin D supplementation can contribute to maintaining healthy teeth and gums. Moreover, vitamin D's anti-inflammatory and other functions may foster not only improved dental health but overall body health. In addition, adequate vitamin D levels may prevent or treat oral cancer.

Finally, the next section comprises the Vitamin D Wellness Protocol.

THE VITAMIN D WELLNESS PROTOCOL

Due to our modern lifestyles and conventional medical practices, we tend to get little vitamin D from its natural source, the ultraviolet B, or UVB, sun rays. From living, commuting, and working indoors to fretfully slapping sunscreen all over our skin, we appear intent on denying ourselves this essential nutrient. As most diets are severely lacking in vitamin D, the most practical way of getting adequate vitamin D is by taking an inexpensive daily, oral D3 supplement as well as vitamin K2, and magnesium.

By following the Vitamin D Wellness Protocol, my vitamin D level has been optimal (greater than or equal to 100 ng/mL (250 nmol/L)) for years. The health benefits described in this book speak for themselves.

The Vitamin D Wellness Protocol

Tens of thousands of people have accessed the three-nutrient, Vitamin D Wellness Protocol on my website: smilinsuepubs.com. Here is the Protocol in a nutshell:

Vitamin D: Most diets do not contain adequate vitamin D. Start by taking 5,000 IU *daily* of vitamin D3 oil-based (soft gels or liquid) supplements with or right after your breakfast. After the first week, take 10,000 IU a day. Enjoy direct noon sun exposure for up to 15-20 minutes a day, when possible.

Vitamin K2: A vitamin K2 diet includes lots of grass-fed meat and dairy products. Since most of us are lacking a daily, abundant intake of grass-fed foods, supplement with about 100 mcg of non-soy vitamin K2 MK-7. Take your K2 and D3 together with, or right after, your breakfast that includes healthy fats such as egg yolks, cottage cheese, other cheeses, avocado, and nuts. NOTES: 1) *Please do not take any form of vitamin K if you are on blood-thinning medication without the approval of your health care practitioner.* 2) If you are taking thyroid medication, avoid taking a *soy*-based, e.g., natto, vitamin K2 MK-7. Soy may disrupt the efficacy of thyroid hormone medication. An alternative to soy is vitamin K2 MK-7 that is derived from fermented chickpeas.

Magnesium: Magnesium-rich foods include leafy green vegetables such as spinach, legumes, avocado, nuts, seeds, and dark chocolates. A *daily* supplement of magnesium glycinate (or magnesium malate) of 400 to 600 mg should boost your levels of this essential mineral. Take your magnesium glycinate before bedtime as the glycine in this supplement has a calming effect that should foster sleep. On the other hand, magnesium malate should be taken in the morning as it may induce energy.

PLEASE NOTE: Persons taking thyroid medication should wait at least *four* hours before taking any magnesium or other mineral supplements.

Concluding Thoughts

Well, there you have it: the easy-to-follow Vitamin D Wellness Protocol. I wish you much success with improved health!

CONCLUDING THOUGHTS

As I conclude writing *Defend Your Life III*, I want to shout from the rooftop, "Vitamin D is essential to our health and quality of life!" We know that virtually every cell in our body contains a vitamin D receptor. When these receptors are activated by a sufficient intake of vitamin D, good things happen to our immune system and overall health.

We also know that vitamin D's functions include anti-viral, anti-cancer, and anti-inflammatory purposes. So, as the COVID-19 pandemic encircled its way across the globe in 2020, I began researching the scientific literature to ascertain if there was any connection between vitamin D and COVID-19. Two years later the science indicates that enjoying adequate vitamin D status may decrease the risk of developing the dreaded coronavirus as well as possibly treating this highly contagious virus.

Defend Your Life III is my third (and probably final) book about vitamin D's health benefits. I encourage you to spread the word about this amazing vitamin.

I hope you have found the information in this book helpful to attain your health goals. Take care.

~Sue

P.S. If you found the information in *Defend Your Life III* useful, please consider posting a positive rating and/or brief review on Amazon. Thank you.

ADDITIONAL RESOURCES

Books

Multiple Sclerosis and (lots of) Vitamin D: My Eight-Year Treatment with The Coimbra Protocol for Autoimmune Diseases by Ana Claudia Domene. 2016. Paper and electronic copies are available via Amazon.

Defend Your Life (2013) *and Defend Your Life II* (2019) by Susan Rex Ryan. Paper and electronic copies are available via Amazon.

Immune. Dettmer, Philipp. Random House. 2021. Hardcover and electronic copies are available via Amazon.

On Immunity. Bliss, Eula. Graywolf Press. 2015. Paperback and electronic copies are available via Amazon.

Silent Inheritance: Are You Predisposed to Depression? by Susan Rex Ryan. 2017. Paper and electronic copies are available via Amazon.

Embrace the Sun: Are You Dying in the Dark? by Marc B. Sorenson and William B. Grant. 2018. Paper copy is available via Amazon.

Websites

Website: www.smilinsuepubs 'dot' com. The author's website and blog.

Website: www.grassrootshealth 'dot' net. Vitamin D-related information.

Website: www.CoimbraProtocol 'dot' com. Lots of information on the Coimbra Protocol and the doctors who treat patients with it.

In addition, vitamin D organizations can be found globally via an Internet search; I recall these countries include Canada, Pakistan, and the United Kingdom.

BIBLIOGRAPHY

Annweiler, G. et al. "Vitamin D Supplementation Associated to Better Survival in Hospitalized Frail Elderly COVID-19 Patients: The GERIA-COVID Quasi-Experimental Study." *Nutrients.* 2020 Nov 2;12(11):3377.

Balla, M. et al. "Back to Basics: Review on Vitamin D and respiratory viral infection including COVID-19." *Journal of Community Hospital Internal Medicine Perspective.* 2020 Oct 29;10(6):529-536.

Biss, Eula. *On Immunity.* Graywolf Press. 2014.

Bocheva, G. et al. "The Impact of Vitamin D on Skin Aging." *International Journal of Molecular Science.* 2021 Aug 23;22(16):9097.

Borsche, L. et al. "COVID-19 Mortality Risk Correlates Inversely with Vitamin D3 Status, and a Mortality Rate Close to Zero Could Theoretically Be Achieved at 50 ng/mL 25(OH)D3: Results of a Systematic Review and Meta Analysis." *Nutrients.* 2021 Oct 14;13(10):3596.

Botelho, J., Machado, V. et al. "Vitamin D Deficiency and Oral Health: A Comprehensive Review." *Nutrients.* 2020 May 19.

Correa-Rodriquez, M. et al. "Vitamin D Levels are Associated with Disease Activity and Damage Accrual in Systemic Lupus Erythematosus Patients." *Biological Research for Nursing.* 2021Jul;23(3):455-463.

Daneels, L. et al. "Maternal Vitamin D and Newborn Telomere Length." *Nutrients.* 2021 Jun 11;13(6):2012.

Dettmer, Philipp. *Immune.* Random House, 2021.

Elamir, A. et al. "A randomized pilot study using calcitriol in hospitalized COVID-19 patients." *Bone.* 2022 Jan;154:116175.

Fahti, N. et al. "Role of vitamin D and vitamin D receptor (VDR) in oral cancer." *Biomedicine & Pharmacotherapy.* 2019 Jan;109:391-401.

Gandi, F. et al. "Impact of vitamin D Supplementation on Multiple Sclerosis." *Cureus.* 2021 Oct 5;13(10):e18487.

Grant, William B. "Review of Recent Advances in Understanding the Role of Vitamin D in Reducing Cancer Risk: Breast, Colorectal, Prostate, and Overall Cancer." *Anticancer Research.* 2020 Jan;40(1):491-499.

Habibi, N. et al. "Maternal diet and offspring telomere length: a systematic review." *Nutritional Reviews.* 2021 Jan 9;79(2):148-159.

Hossain, S. et al. "Vitamin D and breast cancer: A systematic review and meta-analysis of observational studies." *Clinical Nutrition ESPEN.* 2019 Apr;30:170-184.

Ismailova, Aiten. and White, John H. "Vitamin D, infections and immunity." *Reviews in Endocrine and Metabolic Disorders.* 2021 July 29;1-13.

Karonova, TL. et al. "Low 25(OH)D Is Associated with Severe Course and Poor Prognosis in COVID-19." *Nutrients.* 2021 Aug 29;13(9):3021.

Katz, J. et al. "Increased risk for COVID-19 in patients with vitamin D deficiency." *Nutrition.* 2021 Apr;111106.

Kawashima, H. et al. "Serum 25-Hydroxy Vitamin D levels in Japanese Infants with Respiratory Syncytial Virus Infection Younger than 3 Months of Age." *Japanese Journal of Infectious Diseases.* 2020 Nov 24;73(6):443-446.

Li, B et al. "Association between serum vitamin D and chronic rhinosinusitis: a meta-analysis." *Brazilian Journal of Otorhinolaryngology.* 2021 March-April;87(2):178-187.

Mailhot, Genevieve and White, John H. "Vitamin D and Immunity in Infants and Children." *Nutrients.* 2020 Apr 27;12(5):1233.

Meghil, M. et al. "The influence of vitamin D supplementation in local and systemic inflammatory markers in periodontitis patients: A pilot study." *Journal of Randomized Controlled Clinical Trials*. 2019 Jul;25(5):1403-1413.

Papadimitriou, DT. et al, "Association between population vitamin D status and SARS-CoV-2 related serious-critical illness and deaths: An ecological integrative approach." *World Journal of Virology*. 2021 May 25;10(3):111-129.

Patel, MH. et al. "Prophylactic and Therapeutic Role of Vitamin D Supplementation in COVID-19: A Review." *European Journal of Medical and Health Sciences*. 2021 Jul 27.

Pittas, AG, et al. "Vitamin D Supplementation for Prevention of Type 2 Diabetes Mellitus: To D or Not to D?" *Journal of Clinical Endocrinology & Metabolism*. 2020 Dec 1;105(12):3721-3733.

Shimizu, Y. et al. "Intake of 25-Hydroxyvitamin D3 May Reduce the Severity of Upper Respiratory Tract Infection: Post hoc Analysis of a Randomized, Double-Blind, Placebo-Controlled, Parallel Group Comparison Study." *Nutrients*. 2020 Dec 8;12:3769.

Silva, C.C. et al. "Serum levels of vitamin D and Dental Caries in 7-Year-Old Children in thee Porto Metropolitan Area." *Nutrients*. 2021 Jan 7;13(1):166.

Sukharani, N. et al. "Association Between Rheumatoid Arthritis and Serum Vitamin D Levels." *Cureus*. 2021 Sep 24;13(9):e18255.

Sung, H. et al. "Global Cancer Statistics 2020: GLOBOCAN Estimates of Incidence and Mortality Worldwide for 36 Cancers in 185 Countries." *CA: A Cancer Journal for Clinicians*. 2021;71:209-249.

Tabatabaeizadeh, Seyed-Amir and Tafazoli, Niayesh. "The role of vitamin D in prevention of type 2 diabetes. A meta-analysis." *European Society for Clinical Nutrition and Metabolism*. 2021 Feb;41:88-93.

Taha, Rbab et al. "The Relationship Between Vitamin D and Infections Including COVID-19: Any Hopes?" *International Journal of General Medicine*. 2021 Jul 24;14:3849-3870.

Vaghari-Tabari, M. et al. "Vitamin D in respiratory viral infections: a key immune modulator?" *Critical Reviews in Food Science and Nutrition*. 2021 Sep 2;1-16.

Voutsadakis, Ioannis A. "Vitamin D baseline levels at diagnosis of breast cancer: A systematic review and meta-analysis." *Hematology/Oncology and Stem Cell Therapy*. 2021 Mar;14(1):16-26.

Wagner, Carol L. and Hollis, Bruce W. "Early Life Effects of Vitamin D: A Focus on Pregnancy and Lactation." *Annals of Nutrition and Metabolism*. 2020 Nov 24; 76(suppl 2):16-28.

Wei, D. et al. "Vitamin D: Promises on the Horizon and Challenges Ahead for Fighting Pancreatic Cancer." *Cancers*. 2021 May 31;13(1):2716.

Xu, Y. et al. "The effect of vitamin D on the occurrence and development of colorectal cancer: a systematic review and meta-analysis." *International Journal of Colorectal Disease*. 2021 Jul;36(7):1329-1344.

Yildiz M. et al. "The prognostic significance of vitamin D deficiency in patients with COVID-19 pneumonia." *Bratislava Medical Journal*. 2021;122(10):744-747.

Zakhary, CM. et al. "Protective Role of Vitamin D Therapy in Diabetes Mellitus Type II." *Cureus Journal of Medical Science*. 2021 Aug 20;13(8):e17317.

Zarei, M. et al. "The Relationship Between Vitamin D and Telomere/Telomerase: A Comprehensive Review." *Journal of Frailty & Aging*. 2021;10(1):2-9.

INDEX

D

E

G

H

I

K

L

M

N

O

P

Q

R

S

T

U

V

W

Z

GLOSSARY

1,25-dihydroxyvitamin D (1,25(OH)2D): a vitamin D test that measures activated vitamin D. This test is not recommended for reasons stated in Chapter 4.

7-dehydrocholesterol: a chemical produced in the skin when exposed to UVB rays.

25-hydroxyvitamin D (25(OH)D): the gold standard for testing circulating vitamin D or calcidiol.

AMA: American Medical Association, headquartered in Chicago, Illinois.

Antibody: B-cell receptor. (Antibodies are depicted as those red objects on the book cover.)

Antigen: "a piece of an enemy that [your] immune system can recognize."

Antiserum: blood serum that contains antibodies against specific antigens.

B-Cell: an immune cell that slows down and neutralizes pathogens by producing antibodies.

Boron: a little-known element that partners with vitamin D.

CAC: a non-invasive test called "CT coronary artery calcium" scoring.

Calcidiol: circulating vitamin D in the blood.

Calcium: the most abundant mineral in the body that builds and maintains strong bones.

Calcitriol: activated vitamin D in the cells.

CDC: the Centers for Disease Control and Prevention, headquartered in Atlanta, Georgia.

Cholecalciferol: vitamin D3.

Common cold: a highly contagious, respiratory illness caused by other viruses including coronaviruses.

COVID-19: the highly contagious coronavirus that has caused a pandemic since early 2020.

Cytokines: cell signaling molecules that foster immune cell-to-cell communications. Also leads immune cells toward inflammation and infection.

Ergocalciferol: vitamin D2, a less effective form of vitamin D.

Glucose: blood sugar.

Glycosides: chemicals used in some heart medications, e.g., digoxin.

Influenza: highly contagious, respiratory virus that can result in death.

IU: international unit, a common form of measurement of vitamin D supplements.

Lupus: a chronic autoimmune disease that causes pain, swelling, and stiffness in the joints.

Lymphocytes: "natural killer" white blood cells such as B- and T-cells.

Macrophages: large white blood cells that fight pathogens.

Magnesium: a nutritional, chemical element that partners with vitamin D.

Menaquinone: vitamin K2.

MS: a chronic autoimmune disease that could result in death.

Myelin sheath: multiple layers of fatty tissue that surround and protect the nerves including the brain and the nervous system.

Natto: fermented soybeans that are rich in vitamin K2 MK-7.

Neutrophils: front-line white blood cells that surround and capture pathogens.

Oropharyngeal cancer: oral cancer.

Parathyroid: four tiny glands that help to regulate calcium levels by releasing parathyroid hormone or PTH. Parathyroid glands are located behind the thyroid gland.

Pathogen: any invader of the immune system that can cause illness.

Periodontitis: inflammation of the gums.

Phosphorus: a mineral (also referred to as phosphate) that interacts with vitamin D, calcium, and PTH.

Phylloquinone: vitamin K1.

RA: rheumatoid arthritis is an autoimmune disease where the immune system attacks the joint lining, causing inflammation.

RBC Magnesium: a more accurate magnesium test than the serum magnesium blood test. The RBC version measures magnesium in red blood cells.

Rhinosinusitis: persistent inflammation of the sinus and nasal cavities.

RSV: respiratory syncytial virus; highly contagious.

SARS: severe acute respiratory syndrome. COVID-19 is a SARS disease.

SARS-Cov-2: medical term for COVID-19.

SLE: systematic lupus erythematosus, or lupus.

Sunscreen: chemical substances designed to protect the skin by blocking the penetration of UVB A and B rays.

T1DM: type 1 diabetes mellitus, a chronic autoimmune disease where the pancreas does not produce sufficient insulin.

T2DM: type 2 diabetes mellitus, largely a lifestyle disease, where the pancreas produces too much insulin.

T-Cell: an immune cell that targets and attacks a pathogen.

Telomere: a cap on the end of each chromosome that protects DNA.

Ultraviolet B rays: invisible rays that come primarily from sunlight. A moderate exposure (15-20 minutes) around noon may initiate vitamin D production.

URTI: upper respiratory tract infection.

VDR: vitamin D receptors is the protein that allows the cells to take in activated vitamin D.

Vitamin A: a fat-soluble nutrient required in small quantities to support metabolism. Vitamin A also is a partner with vitamin D.

Vitamin K1: a vital, blood-clotting nutrient that recycles in the body.

Vitamin K2: a vitamin D partner nutrient that facilitates moving calcium to the bones and teeth.

Vitamin K2 MK-4: a form of vitamin K2 that is found in grass-fed foods.

Vitamin K2 MK-7: a form of vitamin K2 that is found in some soy products.

WHO: World Health Organization, headquartered in Geneva, Switzerland.

Zinc: an essential trace element that supports the immune system and is a cofactor of vitamin D.

ACKNOWLEDGMENTS

Defend Your Life III would not exist without the incredible research that has been published on vitamin D and its potential health benefits. I thank the dozens of researchers and scientists who are as passionate about exploring vitamin D's role in human health as I am.

Thank you to those who lead non-profit organizations that educate the public about vitamin D including Carole Baggerly of Grassroots Health, and Perry Holman of Canada's Vitamin D Society.

Special thanks to my husband Dave who reviewed my draft work to make it better for you, the reader.

The cover and interior design of *Defend Your Life III* are products of an outstanding graphic design professional named Shannon Bodie of BookWise Design in Oregon. The visual magic created by Shannon and her team enhances the theme of this book.

Much gratitude to the administrators of the Vitamin D Wellness support group on Meta (Facebook). The admin team tirelessly responds to daily questions and offers lots of support to the tens of thousands of Vitamin D Wellness members.

ABOUT THE AUTHOR

Susan "Sue" Rex Ryan was born and raised in Pennsylvania. She earned a Bachelor of Science degree at Georgetown University. Sue also holds a Master of Science degree from the U.S. military's National War College in Washington, D.C. She has earned scores of Continuing Medical Education, or CME, credits from accredited U.S. medical programs approved by, *inter alia*, The American Academy of Family Physicians.

Sue is the author of the popular *Defend Your Life* vitamin D health books. Her debut book won a prestigious Mom's Choice Award®, an international awards program that recognizes authors and others for their efforts in creating quality family-friendly media products.

Defend Your Life II highlights vitamin D's role during the beginning of life as well as research on various ailments that are associated with vitamin D deficiency. This book is dedicated to the Meta Vitamin D Wellness group that Sue founded in 2015.

Defend Your Life III completes the vitamin D trilogy and is Sue's fifth health-related book. The centerpiece of *Defend Your Life III* focuses on vitamin D and immunity, an important topic that needs to gain more public health awareness. In addition, the book reviews the basics of vitamin D and its partners as well as topics including anti-aging and common cancers.

Sue and her husband Dave reside in the sunny suburbs of Las Vegas, Nevada. They enjoy traveling to visit family and friends, as well as experiencing different cultures in far-flung locations including Easter Island, French Polynesia, Qatar, and Sri Lanka.

Sue welcomes your visit to her website—smilinsuepubs.com—that is replete with her blog articles about health topics. You can also follow her on social media including Twitter @VitD3Sue and Instagram "susanrexryan."

Made in the USA
Coppell, TX
18 September 2022